Contents

CLASSIC FESTIVAL SOLOS, Volume 2 is a counterpart to the companion, Volume 1. Idiomatic solo materials with an eye to variety and playability are included, beginning with easier material and progressing to more difficult.

Works from several periods of composition are presented to give the advancing student the opportunity to learn and to demonstrate performance in each appropriate style. Technical progression is taken into consideration as well as program appeal for both soloist and audience.

Jack Lamb, Editor

LITTLE PIECE

ROBERT SCHUMANN
Edited by DAVID SHIFRIN
Arranged by FRANK ERICKSON

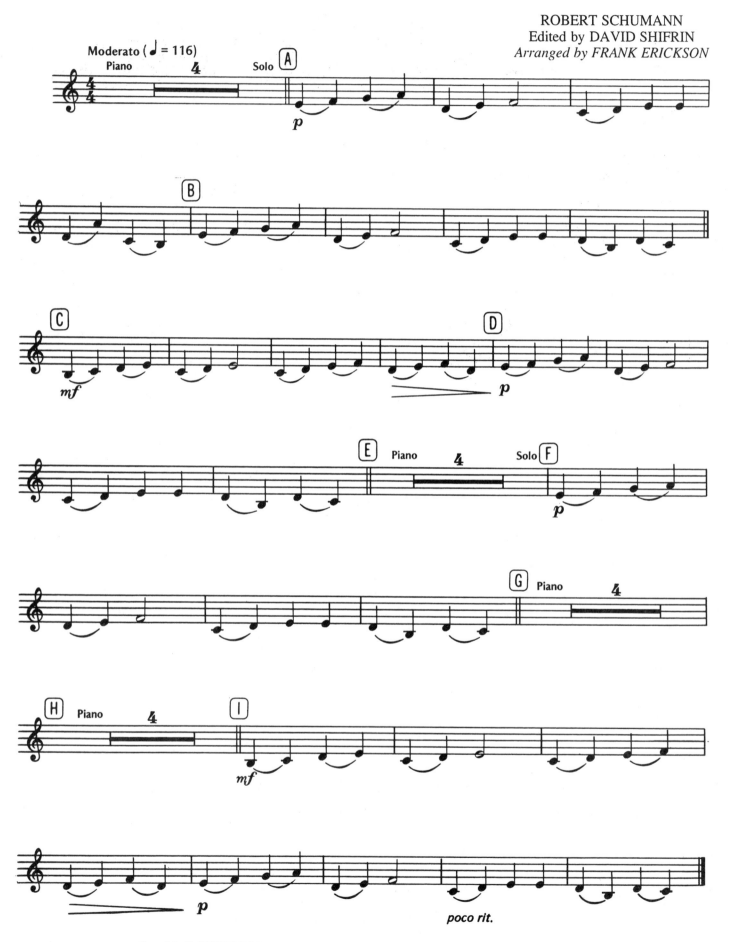

VALSE GRAZIOSO

Nilo W. Hovey & Beldon Leonard

CONCERT PIECE

Suggestions for interpretation: Except for indicated retards the tempo throughout should be a very moderate two beats to the measure. If you have a metronome, set it at 108; if not, consult your teacher. From 5 to 29 and 72 to the end, the quarter notes should be semi-detached . . . . never a full *staccato.* From 33 to 70, the style should be somewhat more *legato* and the quarter notes will be longer. Give careful attention to all marks of expression. Use correct fingerings as indicated in measures 14, 15, 42, 81 and 82.

NILO W. HOVEY & BELDON LEONARD

5

SCHERZINO

JOACHIM ANDERSON, Op. 55, No. 6
Arranged by GEORGE WALN

EL03873

7

BAGATELLE

NILO W. HOVEY & BELDON LEONARD

"Bagatelle" is frequently used for a short, light piece of music, usually, although not always, composed for a key-board instrument such as piano.

Here are some tips for the soloist: All F#'s that are marked "Ch" should be taken with the chromatic F# fingering. Play the number *lightly* throughout .... the crescendos should be made with restraint. The rhythmic figure of an eighth and two sixteenths, which opens the composition, should be played in semi-staccato style, shortening the eighth in keeping with the tempo and indicated style.

9

FOLKSONG FOR CLARINET

ROBERT SCHUMANN
Arranged by GEORGE R. BELDEN

Note: The quarter note triplet pattern may be changed to ♩ ♪♪ if it is too advanced.

PRELUDE

ARMAS JARNEFELT
Arranged by ROBERT LOWRY

EL03873

LA CZARINE
Mazurka

LOUIS GANNE
Arranged by HOVEY-LEONARD

The composer Ganne is perhaps best known for two marches, *Father of Victory*, and *Marche Lorraine*, which attained national prominence in France equal to the popularity of Sousa's *Stars and Stripes Forever* in the United States. However, he composed over 200 other works which are light in character like the Mazurka, *La Czarine*.

Some suggestions for the soloist . . . . the predominant figure of an eighth note, sixteenth rest and sixteenth note must be played crisply, in full staccato style; optional octaves are indicated from measures 15 to 19 and 47 to 51 . . . . use the register that sounds best; *the trill of measure 26 should be executed by using the regular "A" fingering and trilling the top side key on the right side;* the Bb's in measures 59, 60, 63, 96, 97 and 100 should be taken with the side fingering for clarity of tone.

D.C. al Fine

EL03873

13

STAR FALL

GEORGE R. BELDEN

Copyright © 1978 BELWIN MILLS PUBLISHING CORP., c/o CPP/BELWIN, INC., Miami, FL 33014

WALTZ FROM "COPPELIA"

DELIBES
Arranged by HOVEY-LEONARD

Although we would not wish to vouch for the authenticity of the story, it has been said that Fritz Kreisler actually composed this delightful waltz tune when he was still a very young boy. Delibes, impressed with the melody, asked for and obtained permission to use it in the ballet "Coppelia" which he was writing at the time.

Here are some fingering tips for the soloist . . . . . in measure **13**, the F♯ should be played with the chromatic fingering; in measure **18**, the A♯ will usually sound better if played with the side key fingering; in measures **33** and **34**, you will save some excess finger motion by leaving the fingers of the right hand on while playing the B♭'s and the A; the trill in measure **60** should be executed by using the regular fingering for D♯ and trilling only the third finger of the right hand; third line B natural in measures **63, 64** and **65** may be played with the right side B, but this is not absolutely essential.